MIREILLE DE REILHAN

AGATEWARE POTTERY MAGIC

ANDRE DEUTSCH

ULISSEDITIONS

First published in Great Britain in 1995 by
André Deutsch Limited
106 Great Russell Street, London WC1B 3LJ

Copyright © Ulisse Editions 1995
15 rue de Prony, 92600 Asnières – France

General Editor: John Tittensor
Photos: Peter Maidment
Layout: Mario Giamar
Photocomposition: Comp2, Turin
Editing by In-folio, Turin

ISBN 0-233-98942-0

Printed in Hong Kong by Colorcraft

Contents

A selection of agateware pieces by Mireille de Reilhan.

Preface

In almost all the great bodies of mythology, be they oriental or occidental, there exist stories of the genesis of the universe. In these legends we find accounts of the earliest relationships between men and the gods, of the creation of the material universe and of the living species that inhabit that universe. Primitive man is quite literally born out of the earth, shaped by a God who makes him in His own image, who fills him with the breath of life and thus provides him with a soul. And yet at the same time this God destines his human creation – in the twilight of his earthly existence and inasfar as his bodily being is concerned – to return to the basic stuff from which he was made, the primordial clay that is both our cradle and our eternal resting place: 'Dust thou art and unto dust thou shalt return.' To Job, crushed by adversity, the wise man Elihu offers a solemn reminder : 'The spirit of God hath made me… I also am formed out of the clay.' A more insightful translation of the book of Genesis might have gone much more deeply into the question of earth as matter – and of clay in particular, as is the case in the sacred texts of various other religions. And just as the God of the Bible, and the demigods of these other traditions, form men out of this alluvium, this fundamental clay, humankind show its recognition of its origins – and its gratitude – by working in turn in the same material. Men create and have always created likenesses and statues without number, endlessly in search of concrete representations of the Creator, of objects propitious to devotion, to the contemplation of the divine. In other words, this working in clay has always involved an intimate mingling of the sacred and the profane: we can often discern there, as they say in the East, the place where Heaven and Earth meet. But there's another type of meeting taking place too, and a profoundly surprising one: that between the religious tradition and contemporary science. The latest advances in biology have detected RNA and DNA chains in the very heart of this humble clay; it's as if modern science is setting out to explain, to translate into rationalist terminology and experimental knowhow, exactly what the world's great holy books have described in terms of myth. But let's look directly at the uses to which the intrinsic qualities of clay – and by extension the art of ceramics – have given us access. Firstly, from time immemorial clay has revealed to man its therapeutic properties – its capacity to absorb or to arrest the action of various toxins, viruses and bacteria. Let's not forget, either, the high-tech side of things: the use of ceramic materials in advanced medical prostheses and in the American space shuttle. The presence of clay thus spans the centuries, praised by Hippocrates, by Galen, by the apothecaries of the Middle Ages – and by those whose task it is to direct today's schools of medicine.

What touches us above all here is another, totally fascinating kind of meeting: the meeting between the useful and the esthetically pleasing. For what the Greeks called *kerameia* – the technique and the art of working with earth in general – has given rise since the earliest times to works and objects which have played a central role in different civilisations. In some cases the discovery and application of certain techniques in this field has actually generated specific forms of social organization. We have only to think of the architectural role of stamped earth, of adobe – and later of bricks, shaped in moulds and fired. At a very early stage in man's history, the making of pottery objects made possible the storing and the transport of various foods and liquids – a development which radically changed man's relationship not only with the natural world, but also with his fellow human

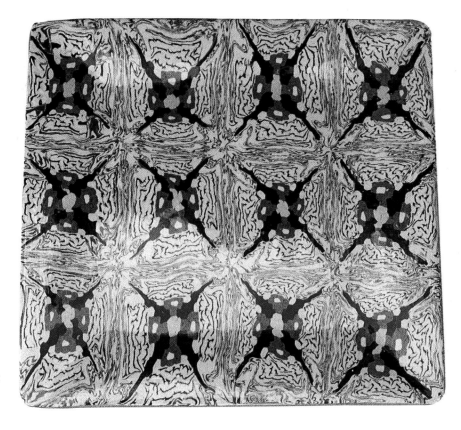

For this ashtray the author has used a repeated geometric pattern.

beings, in social and commercial terms. What is surprising here is that these primitive objects – Amerindian, African, Asian and so on – which today most of us accept as inherently beautiful, only possessed at the beginning what André Malraux termed 'chance beauty'. In other words, for the makers of these objects, function was the major preoccupation. It was not until much later that craftsman set out consciously to produce works of art, that is to say, objects for which their primary concern was the use of form and colour. And yet, well before this esthetic quest took deliberate form, working with clay was held – in the great majority of cultures where it was practised – to be a noble activity. This was purely and simply because it allowed a marked improvement in the quality of daily life, at both the individual and collective levels. Once the esthetic dimension appeared, however, it did not take long for this kneading of clay – let's not forget that its preparation calls for a kneading akin to that of dough by a baker – to take on an almost sacred character. This was because the work of art could be considered as true spiritual nourishment both for its creator and for

the person contemplating it. The work of art nourishes the spirit just as bread nourishes the body. And just as, in the course of time, bread would in certain instances become so sacred as to incarnate the body of the Divinity, so it was for the working of clay. This was a truly Promethean activity, releasing out of the most simple of raw materials the shapes and colours dreamed by the artist.

Bread and clay: a parallel that merits thinking about. In the Middle Ages, during periods of shortage, it was common practice for bakers to mix clay into their flour: the very earth thus became a source of nourishment. And this 'earth-eating' is something we find in

all cultures and in all ages. But to come back to the business of working with clay: it's interesting that ceramicists don't refer to themselves as artists, preferring the term 'craftsmen'.

It's as if they want to put the emphasis on the manual aspect of what they do, on the gradual domestication of a highly resistant – and sometimes even hostile – raw material, a material that has to be tamed, patiently. It's as if they want to stress the technical mastery their profession demands – a mastery which goes hand in hand with the quest for beauty they've set out on.

When we talk about this openly spiritual search – one so closely allied to the rigorous acquisition of a body of knowledge – we find ourselves face to face with Moroccan, Balinese and Indian potters: men with mystic souls and the hands of peasants. In these men too, Heaven and Earth come together. A question of fervour, then, and of a certain gravity of approach – but with a touch of humour and much more than a touch of real tenderness. All these qualities are to be found in Mireille de Reilhan – and her works too are shot through with them.

It would seem that in her work with clay and in ceramics, she has been able to bring together in a highly productive way the different forms of questioning she had undertaken, the different paths she had explored before consecrating herself wholly to her chosen art form: paths that had led her through painting, sculpture, collage, advertising graphics, fabric design for one of France's leading couturiers and other creative fields. But it is in ceramics that she finds, in addition to the possibility of using these diverse artistic abilities, a direct, sensual confrontation with her material. This development was linked to her return to a tiny Provençal village, after many years spent living in Morocco and in other parts of her native France; a return that was to lead to the discovery of all those clays – monochrome, marbled, veined, streaked, iridescent – that enrich the geology of the Mediterranean countries and which seem to give concrete expression to the special quality of the light of Provence. Her return also helped her to find the ideal geographical setting for the work that was to come. Amongst this work we find vases of generous proportions, others possessed of the abstract purity of a cubist drawing, and surfaces as simple as the canvases of certain painters: her plates, dishes, ashtrays are no more than pretexts for the endless development of that graphic richness which so many Japanese and American collectors have found so irresistible; and which has earned her work a place in the Christian Dior boutique in Paris and in the French capital's Museum of Decorative Arts.

It could be said that sometimes her influences – allusions might be a better word here – are fairly obvious, at least inasfar as certain of her themes are concerned: her use of sunflowers and irises is a clear example. But it's never a question of imitation – what's involved is, rather, exploration and appropriation. The name Van Gogh could justifiably be invoked in this regard, but her work also calls to mind Vasarely and Delaunay. And when we come face to face with her marbled motifs – so warm, so dense – the landscapes of North Africa, of Mali and of Mauretania are never far away. This is not imitation, then, but rather the direct expression of emotions triggered by a voyage, an exhibition or a landscape glimpsed some summer evening, when the heat-saturated air is vibrant with the colours of flowers and trees.

We have already noted the resistance of clay to our attempts at mastery. In addition, the practice of agateware demands an extraordinarily high degree of technical skill. In the work of Mireille de Reilhan we find an enormous graphic richness, an intensity and warmth in certain colours that contrasts with the diaphanous and almost other-worldly delicacy of others, a delicious airiness that she accentuates via her choice of motifs: evanescent butterflies, sumptuous fish come from the limpid waters of Polynesian lagoons.

Another fine ceramicist, Ayca Riedinger, points out in her book that working with clay involves the four elements that so many of the traditional cosmogonies make reference to: earth, air, fire and water. Nothing could be more evident in the ceramic creations of Mireille de Reilhan: not only in the choice of the very special technique we call agateware, in the preparation the clays demand, in the manner of their firing – but also in respect of the pictorial qualities of these works, which present themselves to us as a concrete manifestation of the elements, as the bringing together of all their force and plastic beauty. There's a kind of alchemy at work here – or magic, as she prefers to say when she speaks of her work. And out of this alchemy emerges the universe of Mireille de Reilhan, a universe of infinite poetry.

Alain Perraud

1. Historical Background

The making of agateware – ceramic pieces created from carefully prepared and stained clays – is practised by very few potters. This is at least in part because of the specific problems and the relatively high level of uncertainty the technique involves. Firstly, agateware demands an extremely slow and meticulous way of working. Secondly, the degree of shrinkage during drying and firing is far from predictable, and this gives rise to a failure rate that is considerably higher than for the more 'standard' pottery techniques. Then there's the question of the designs used on the pieces and of the colour relationships: you can never be sure exactly what you're going to come up with at the end of the process. On the other hand, there's the incredible richness and variety of the designs, and the sumptuousness of the colours: the sheer beauty of a piece that works from beginning to end makes you understand why certain potters get 'hooked', in spite of the difficulties.

The potters of the East – the Chinese and the Japanese – have long since mastered all the major aspects of this technique.

In China we find marbled motifs in popular pottery from the 7th Century onwards: what was involved at this early stage was putting together slabs, strips or fragments of coloured clay, using the natural colours of the various clays local potters had at their disposal. During the Sung Dynasty, from the 10th to the 13th Century, Chinese potters were still making extensive – and highly esthetic – use of marbling in their creation of such everyday objects as goblets, bowls, perfume-braziers, paperweights and so on. Then there came a change; and up until the 20th Century, these past masters of

A checkerboard-and-stripe plate.

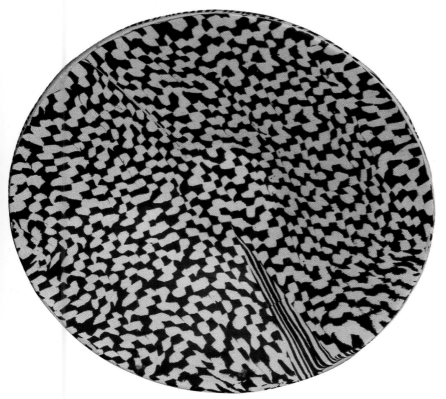

the ceramic art devoted their attention to refining their skills in the areas of porcelain and stoneware. They abandoned the deliberate colouring of their clays, putting the emphasis on the delicate translucidity of their porcelain and on surface decoration using highly subtle brush-drawing techniques. Agateware came to France in the 18th century, when Claude-François Moulin (b. 1738) and Jacques Barthélemy (b. 1741), opened their workshop in Apt in 1768. It is to these two potters that we in France owe the introduction of the type of fine china still called 'porphyry' or 'portor', after the kinds of marble its patterns resemble. Using clays that had been stained to get a marbled effect, the two French pioneers imitated the agate-style fine china produced in England since the 1740s by Josiah Wedgwood and Thomas Whieldon.

In France, this particular technique was later taken up by the potters of Orléans and Sarreguemines; of Douai in the north; of Thuin (near Perpignan, in the south) in the 19th Century; and by Pichon, in Uzès, at the beginning of the 20th Century. It is probably true to say that Apt is now the major French – and maybe European – agateware centre. But it was in Castellet, around 1728, that César Moulin had the idea of trying out new combinations of the red, green, brown and white clays that enriched the soil in the vicinity of majestic Mount Ventoux. Later these same vividly coloured clays would appear in the works of many famous landscape painters.

Thus it was that the traditional yellow pottery of the time found itself ousted, in terms of public esteem, by the new multicoloured pieces.

And this was no transitory situation: even today there are still plenty of potters who devote themselves exclusively to this way of working.

The lasting success of this particular style has not, however, deterred various craftsmen from trying to enlarge the range of colourings and patterns. They have done this by using metallic oxydes as additional colouring agents and by extending their approach to include such variations as inlay-work. We'll talk more about this further on in the book.

Mireille de Reilhan, Fish *(1993).*

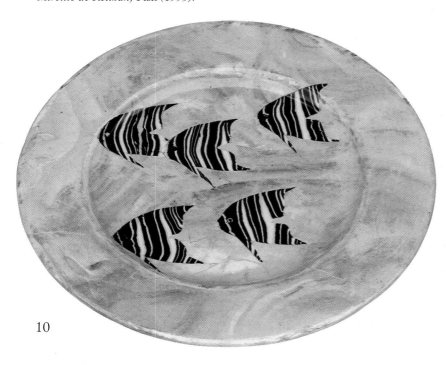

2. Agateware: Pottery Magic

For me there is quite simply nothing more fascinating or more magical than to be able to mingle my clays at will in the way the agateware technique allows. I'm in a totally different situation from a lot of other potters, who don't get to see results until the very last stages of their work on a piece – and sometimes not until the piece comes out of the kiln. In the case of agateware the pleasure is immediate: for me it begins the moment I start to choose the colorants I'm going to use. The colour possibilities are there before your very eyes and straight away a kind of very special vibration starts up. It's as if a film is being projected inside your imagination, showing you the colours mingling and contrasting as, in your mind, the object you're going to make begins to take shape. And then you give all this real, concrete expression.

When I talk about magic, what I mean is that at each moment, and with each new manipulation of the clay, I'm involved with colour, with warmth – and with life. It's with these vibrations as a starting point that each creator must learn to express and interpret, to bring forth a work of art.

Mireille de Reilhan, plate (1993). A finely-balanced mixture of marbling and geometrical patterns.

Agateware: the technique

Butterflies *(1992). A delicate, almost ethereal treatment of a simple subject.*

The great majority of ceramic pieces bear some kind of painted decoration. They have been, in other words, ornamented with brushwork or glazed: this latter term means that they've been covered with a fine layer of vitreous liquid, which modifies their colour during firing, via the action on the clay of metallic oxides contained in the glaze. In the case of agateware, the process is altogether different. The colour and/or the design are not simply added to the surface after the making of the initial piece: they are part and parcel of the mass of clay the piece is made of. In other words, the potter working in this field uses clays of different colours to create subtle combinations and to compose the images making up his designs.

The main approaches involve bringing together slabs, strips or small pieces of coloured clay in a mould. A second method is that of inlays: the potter creates decorative shapes in coloured clay, then sets them into the surface of a thin sheet of clay of another colour. The simplest and most accurate parallel is that with the work of the cabinet-maker, when he sets out to create a marquetry design. Working this way gives the creator an enormous range of graphic possibilities; but the process is slow and exacting, and it calls for extreme precision. In spite of all the attention that goes into the preparatory stages, the failure rate during assembly, drying and firing is always high: one major factor here is that the potter is using a variety of different clays, but has to give them all a uniform level of shrinkage. The best way to get this uniformity is to exercise the greatest care in the preparation of the mixtures. This means that rather than using blocks of clay, it is preferable to make up a slip from powdered clay, then add the necessary colourants. Next, the drying process should be as slow as possible. Prior to drying, it is vital that the different elements of a piece contain precisely the same proportion of water. Once dry, the pieces should be rubbed down with a rubber kidney, then sanded back with steel wool or a jex pad. The final phase involves covering the whole piece with a transparent glaze: the idea here is to bring out the vividness of the colours and to define the decorative element as clearly as possible. Before we can sit down and contemplate our finished piece we should return for a moment to our real point of departure: to this inert raw material which, via the inspiration, the virtuosity and the sheer hard work of the ceramicist, is going to be turned into a refined work of art. This raw material is the clay we use – with all its manifold possibilities.

12

Clay

Clay is a raw material that lends itself to many different uses; and this means that when we set out here into the world of ceramics, we really have to have a clear idea of what it is we're looking for, of what it is we want to do. So the task this book sets itself is to talk about a single technique: that of the creation of agateware. Clay can be used to create, to construct, to model, to contain – and even to write on. Think of that famous Egyptian statuette – made of clay – which portrays a seated scribe hard at work: using an engraving tool of hardened clay, he is keeping, on sheets of soft clay, a record of the laws, the works, the legends and the financial affairs of the Pharaoh. Clay has the advantage of being available just about everywhere and in considerable quantities. In addition, getting it out of the ground poses no great problems. This means that it is cheap – and yet its ready availability and its cheapness in no way detract from the esthetic and practical possibilities I've already talked about. It has a highly plastic character, due to its special physico-chemical makeup – it is composed of tiny flakes and crystals. This plasticity is underlined by an inherent water-content: to make it do what we

Mireille de Reilhan: a plate using marbling and floral forms.

want, we begin by simple modifications of the proportion of water a given clay contains.

Clay sources

We find clay in exotic places: at the bottom of lakes, and deep in the sea-bed – but also just about anywhere where the combination of plenty of rain and low temperatures produce the breakdown of rock. Obviously, the rock which is gradually broken down by the elements and the passage of time is not exactly the same everywhere. Thus erosion and the decomposition of the earth's crust produce clays that differ from one place to another. The serious ceramicist has to take this into account, for what's involved are differences not only of colour, but also of chemical composition, of response to the various kinds of handling and drying necessitated by different techniques, and of behaviour during the final stage of firing. When all is said and done, pottery can be divided into its various categories – stoneware, earthenware, porcelain and so on – if the materials are chosen with care, if the proportions used respect the particular characteristics of the different clays and if the firing takes place in the right setting and at the appropriate temperature. This explains why plenty of potters – and especially non-professionals – prefer to buy their clays prepared and ready to use; at least this can help to avoid a lot of unpleasant surprises.

14

3. Some General Observations

The majority of clays are composed of alumina and silica belonging to the felspar family. Mixed with these, we find small quantities of other minerals: quartz, carbon compounds, iron oxyde and many others. The specific character of each clay is thus determined by the differing proportions of the substances that make it up, but we can divide clays as a whole into two main groups: primary and secondary.

1. Primary clays

We find these clays 'on site', that is to say at the very spot where the weathering and disintegration of the rock took place. The commonest – and the best known – of this group is kaolin. The name comes from that of a hill situated near jau Chan Fu, in China: it is here that for centuries men have extracted this very pure clay, source of the world-famous Chinese porcelains.

This purity is in fact the great drawback of kaolin, which is all but unusable in the raw state. Fortunately, mixed in the right proportions with other minerals – notably bentonite – kaolin becomes more workable and retains the two basic qualities needed for the making of porcelain: its toughness and its whiteness.

2. Secondary clays

Here we are dealing with clays which, as a result of various geological phenomena, have been displaced from their place of origin. The main factor involved here is the action of water. These clays have finished up by settling in sedimentary layers – but along the way they have picked up all sorts of impurities: the minerals and fragments of vegetable matter which give each type its special character. Thus we have clays

Fish are one of the author's favorite decorative designs.

15

of different colours, different levels of plasticity, different rates of shrinkage during drying and firing, and so on. These clays are very fine and flaky; they are also highly plastic and thus easy to work. A very common term in this context is 'ball clay' – a name due to the form under which the clay was transported from its source to the pottery works of England at the beginning of the industrial era. The decaying vegetable matter picked up by these clays in the course of their journeyings often give them a black or bluish colour; but when fired, they become white, or take on a most agreeable buff colour.

There is, however, an important non-organic ingredient picked up by these clays on the move: the iron oxide which explains the redness of certain clays.

Primary or secondary, that is the question

Each of the two main types of clay includes a considerable range of variations of colour, texture, plasticity and malleability. The traditional names given to these different clays have several origins:
– those that name the site: montmorillonite, kolinite, illite, attapulgite;
– those that describe their appearance: glauconite, chlorite, vermiculite;
– those that stress a particular property: saponite, smectite;
– those that 'dedicate' the clay to the scientist, the geologist or the artist who first discovered or studied it: halloysite, leverrierite, dickite, etc.
Having said this, most ceramicists are neither chemists, physicists or geologists, and as such they will most often opt for prepared clays with well-defined characteristics.

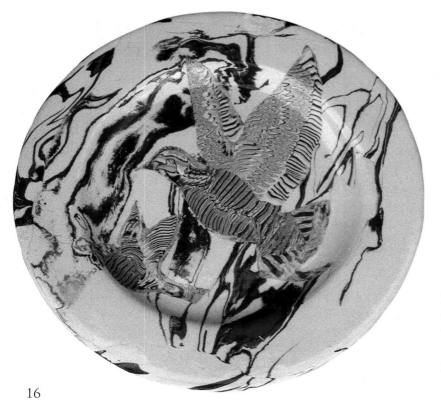

Left: A 'bird plate' by Mireille de Reilhan: a marvellous mingling of striped and marbled clays.

Facing page: *Detail of the bird motif.*

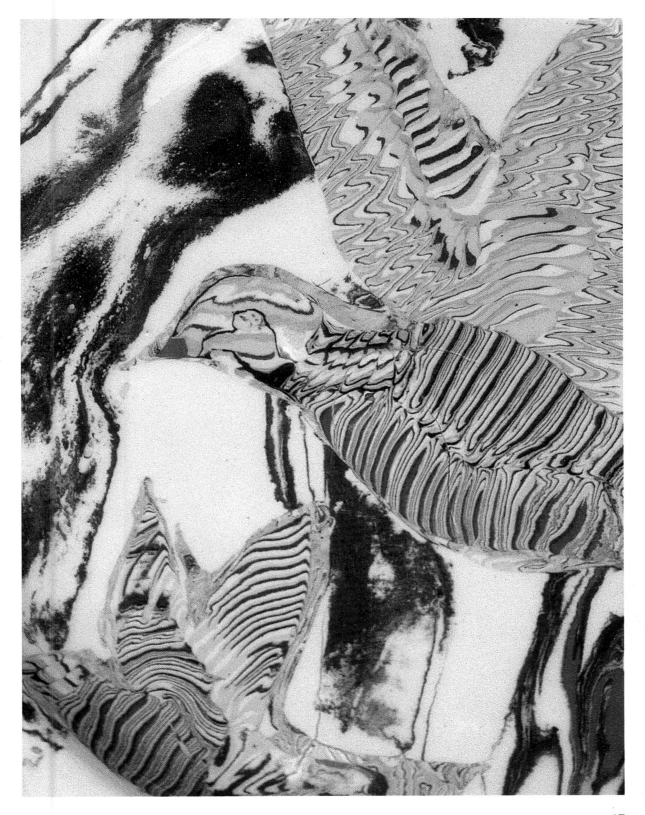

Prepared clays

As every potter knows, good clay, like good wine, improves with age. There are bacteria living in clay, and with the passing of time their presence gives rise to an improved plasticity.

One of the great Taoist potters of China used to say that he was using today the clay he had prepared in a past existence, and that the clay he was in the process of preparing was destined to be used in a future life. Another version of the same story – still in China – takes the form of an adage: the true potter prepares the clay his grandson will use, while making his own pots with the clay handed down to him by his grandfather.

Unlike the people of the Orient, we westerners rarely have the patience and the wisdom to let time do its work.

And so we often find potters artificially speeding up the ageing of the clay they are about to use by mixing in a small quantity of clay which has had time to 'mature'.

There's nothing to stop you doing this, but the longer your prepared clay has waited, the better your results will be.

What exactly is prepared clay?

We all know that when we buy commercial clays in art-supply or specialist shops, they come in the form of malleable blocks

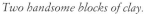

Two handsome blocks of clay.

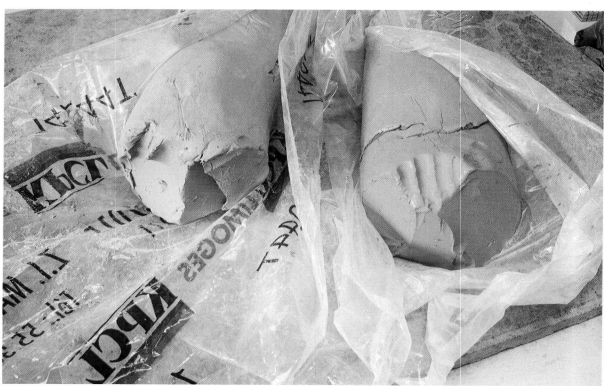

('wads') or bags of powder. In this more or less natural state, they will be grey, buff, red, greenish, brown or white, depending on the proportion of iron they contain.

As far as other colours or other shades of the same colours are concerned it is – as we shall see further on – the addition of different oxydes that counts: each one will have its own specific influence on the colour you end up with after firing. But for the moment we're dealing with the raw clay that we've gone out and bought somewhere – preferably from a specialist.

This will be a ready-to-use clay and we will have chosen it taking two main factors into consideration: its colour and its plasticity. The commonest commercial form of clay is the more or less standard wad of around 10 kilogrammes, wrapped in plastic. But what we're looking for is clay in powder form: later we're going to have to colour it, and opting for powdered clay is going to make this a lot easier.

A useful tip: avoid buying clay in too-large quantities. Buy according to your immediate needs, rather than stocking up big – it's no fun reconstituting clay that has dried out and hardened because it's been stored too long.

As far as plasticity is concerned, we need to distinguish between clays for modelling, for throwing, for turning and for slip-casting. But for our purposes the clays we're going to

A bag of powdered clay, with a packet of deflocculant.

talk about here will be grouped according to their firing temperature. All temperatures are quoted in degrees Celsius.

There are many different kinds of clay, but we can divide them into five main groups:

• *Red clay.* This is the most common of all and the one used for terra cotta pieces. Potters who work with a wheel like its high level of plasticity.
Its firing temperature – from 1000 to 1080 °C – has no effect on the redness of its colour.

• *White clay.* Creamy or pinkish in its raw state, it keeps its initial colour after being fired between 1060 and 1180 °C.

• *Stoneware.* Initially grey, after being fired at between 1200 and 1300 °C it takes on a very attractive buff colour.

• *Soft-paste porcelain.* Despite being described as 'soft', it has a low plasticity and is used mainly for turning.
Firing temperatures go from 1240 to 1260 °C.

• *True porcelain.* Cream-coloured in the raw state, after firing between 1280 and 1350 °C, it becomes the whitest of all the prepared clays.

Wedging a wad of clay takes time and calls for considerable energy.

Wedging

The clay you buy in a shop specialized in potters' supplies is more or less ready to use. Agateware has a tendency to spring unwelcome surprises on the unsuspecting practitioner – and so, if you want to spare yourself a loss of time, you'll need to undertake some additional preparation of your basic material. The crackling and the splitting that are the bane of the potter's existence – especially when he's a beginner – occur mainly during the drying and firing processes. They result from a lack of homegeneity in the raw material used, or sometimes from the presence of air bubbles in the clay. If you opt for non-powdered clay, these air bubbles have *got* to be

eliminated. To do this, you'll have to work your clay vigorously, whack it about a bit and knead it, in the same way as an experienced baker prepares his mass of dough for the oven. And so, first off you'll cut the wad of clay into slices with a wire; each slice will undergo the treatment indicated above, and then you'll reconstitute the wad: now it will be completely homogeneous, not only to look at, but more importantly, in terms of its texture.

Now you'll have to let it rest a little while. And while you're waiting for it to reach the ready-to-use stage, it should be kept in a cool place and wrapped in plastic so the air can't get at it. A humid environment is all to the good here: it will ensure that the clay doesn't dry out.

Choosing your clay

It has already been made clear that in this book we are concentrating on a very specific technique: the preparation and creation of agateware, an area of ceramic creation that is totally different from what the general public calls 'pottery'. Given this precise context, the only clays we can use in the raw state – as far as their colours go – are the reds and the whites: those used for terra cotta production. Their firing temperature is relatively low (see page 19). A word of warning: don't confuse 'white clay' and 'porcelain' – while it's true that the latter is white both before and after its visit to the kiln, its firing temperature is considerably higher and doesn't suit our way of working.

Colours and colour-schemes

The originality of this technique, and what gives it such a varied range of æsthetic possibilities, is the way it pushes the ceramicist towards the discovery of nuance and interplay in the choice and disposition of his colours. Naturally enough, this emphasis on subtlety and finesse must also be reflected in the decorative motifs used. The colours in question are not ones that occur naturally. The task is to create them, using metallic oxydes as colouring agents. Once we choose this approach, the use of powdered clay becomes almost obligatory: obviously it's much easier to colour a liquefied clay, that is to say a 'slip' prepared by dissolving powdered clay in water, than it is in the case of a solid wad. The colouring of the slip presents no real difficulties: a small dose of manganese oxyde or cobalt oxyde can give truly superb results.

The preparation of liquid clay

Let's start with the necessary quantity of powdered white clay. We make our slip by dissolving this clay in water until we get a fluid of the smooth consistency of liquid cream. As a general rule we can say that around 3 litres of water will be about right for 10 or 12 kilos of powdered clay. If possible, an electric 'blunger' is a useful adjunct here. Turning slowly and regularly, it saves you work and ensures a good, even mixture. Having said this, if you're thinking in terms of relatively modest quantities of slip, manual preparation is no great problem – it just takes longer. At all times – and in this the preparation of slip demands exactly the same attention and vigilance as good cooking – you must be on the lookout for 'lumps'. The presence of lumps can be disastrous, but most often the addition of a small sachet of deflocculant to the mix will suffice to ensure a creamy and homogeneous result.

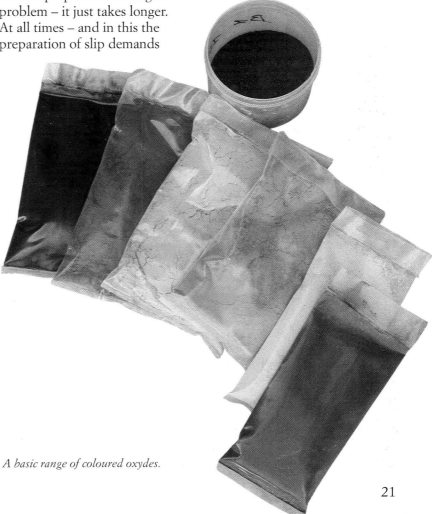

A basic range of coloured oxydes.

Adding the oxydes

The oxydes used for colouring come in the form of different-coloured powders. First off, you dissolve the oxyde in a little water, then you add it to your slip. The exact quantity will depend in each case on the task in hand and the colour you want.

An example. Take a teaspoon of the metallic oxyde and dissolve it in a bowl with a soup-spoon of water. Then pour your slip into the bowl, taking care to mix carefully as you go, until you get a uniformly-coloured liquid.

All you have to do now is let the slip dry out to the point of being usable. A lot of potters simply pour their freshly-coloured slip into a shallow plaster container or onto a sheet of plasterboard. The plaster absorbs part of the water and allows the slip to dry out gradually and evenly.

Once this initial drying process is finished, the coloured clay will have taken on the consistency of fairly supple modelling clay and you will have no trouble lifting it off the drying surface. When you've done this, make the clay into a ball and work it – striking and kneading it – just as you do with a block of normal clay.

Now you're ready to go. Your raw material is there waiting: all that remains is for the artist to use his inspiration and 'lay bare his soul' of the clay.

Preparing the slip: the electric drill is used with a special mixer-bit.

The slip dries in a shallow plaster container.

4. *The Studio and the Tools*

No matter how modest his aspirations at the technical and æsthetic levels, the practitioner of agateware has to come to grips with his material in quite a number of different ways. He's going to have to strike it, wedge it, cut and recut it, flatten it, put it into all sorts of moulds, pour it, scrape it, polish it, paint it, dry it out and – last but not least – 'cook' it at the firing stage. None of this is simple, but none of it is impossible either. The potter simply needs to be aware at the outset that this kind of work, like any other art or craft, makes its own specific demands. He'll need a certain number of tools, some subsidiary equipment – and the right kind of setting: a studio, a workplace, call it what you like.

The ideal workplace

It is always preferable, for the exercise of an artistic or a craft activity, to have a place of work which doesn't get used for anything else. Pottery and ceramics in general are highly physical activities: the moulds used and the objects created are often quite heavy and this weight can mean that handling, moving or using them is not always an easy matter. Especially when we take into account the fragility of certain objects at the various stages of their creation. A sound principle, then, is to handle the materials as little as possible. This means that the ideal workplace, even when it's not especially big, brings all the necessary elements together. The kiln, for example, should not be too far from the workbench and from the tools the making of the pieces requires. The workspace should also be well lit and easy to heat: don't forget that there's always a fair amount of water around and that working in a cold, damp environment in winter is far from agreeable. It's also very useful to have easy access to an outdoor area: there you'll be able to dry your pieces faster and more easily and you'll avoid the problems of dust build-up resulting from the sanding of your creations. You'll need too a cool place to store your bags of clay – somewhere sheltered but at the same time slightly humid, so as to avoid all the problems that go with the drying-out of your clay before you've even used it.

So much for the ideal – but there's no reason why the amateur ceramicist can't work in his own

The studio and the tools.

kitchen! The essential thing is that within the limits of what's possible, the workspace should meet the practical requirements of the craft he has chosen and should satisfy his own tastes. There's nothing more agreeable to be surrounded by one's tools and equipment, one's raw materials, by works in progress and works that have been successfully brought to completion. The potter needs above all the right ambience, an environment conducive to creation and to creative thinking.

Back on the practical level, he'll need, for obvious reasons, a floor that's easy to clean and a tap that's easy to get at – potters need water all the time.

Shelving is another important factor. You need to know where things are, where to find your tools – as well as space for your moulds and for pieces that are finished or still at various stages of creation. In other words, good big shelves and plenty of them.

To return to a point already mentioned, but one which really can simplify your existence once you start to work on a larger scale: an electric blunger will relieve you of the task of preparing your slip and will guarantee a mixture of good, uniform consistency – important considerations both.

As I have already said, the technique of agateware involves making ceramic objects by bringing together strips and pieces of different-coloured clays. By far the greater part of this work will take place on a flat surface. To optimize your work, you will need (ideally) a table with a sheet of marble on it. If this is out of the question, get yourself another good, flat surface: a piece of wood or hardboard that will help in the cutting and assembling of your strips and various other clay shapes.

The tools

Some indispensable tools:

– A wire-and-wood slab-cutter
– Scissors
– Rubber kidney
– Turning tools
– Rolling pin
– Cutting wire
– Knife
– Wooden modelling tool
– Wire-ended modelling tool
– Needle in stick

As for the 'toolkit' needed specifically for agateware, the following are indispensable:

– A cutting wire. This should be of nylon or very thin wire, about 50 cm long, and with a ring or a piece of wood at each end to make it easy to hold.

– A roller, of about the same size as an ordinary rolling pin and preferably of wood.

– A modelling tool.

– Wire-ended modelling tools.

– A banding wheel.

– Rubber kidneys for smoothing down.

– A good sharp cutting knife (or better still, several, of different sizes).

The cutting of the individual pieces before the actual assembly plays a major role in agateware work. The choice of

the tools is up to you, but should include a range of sharp-edged turning tools, ripping-irons (sharpened metal triangles mounted on a wooden handle), and pieces of steel of all shapes and sizes (round, triangular, square) with lightly honed edges. Your capacity for improvisation will come in handy here, since you may be creating shapes whose cutting demands tools that 'don't exist' – you'll have to invent them.

Other handy items:

- A small electric grinding wheel, to keep your cutting instruments up to the mark.
- Natural or synthetic sponges of different sizes and textures.
- Jex pads or steel wool, for rubbing-back.
- Buckets and basins.
- Sieves.
- Glazing tongs.
- An electric drill.

And at the risk of repeating myself, stock up on improvised tools of all types, shapes and sizes. More than any other craft, ceramics involves a constant search for new, practical, cheap ways of doing things and solving technical and artistic problems. Precision and pragmatism: two

of the great (and complementary) virtues in this field.

But perhaps your interest in pottery (in general) or in agateware (in particular) is still slightly tentative and you're wondering about the wisdom of outlaying large sums on tools. In this case, hunt out a specialist shop and ask if they stock a beginner's kit.

Without including everything mentioned in the list above, this kit will provide enough tools – and sound advice on their use – for you to get an idea of whether or not you want to take matters further.

Health and safety

It's time to add a few other items to our list: a protective apron, protective gloves and – above all – an efficient mask with a changeable filter. Breathing in fumes, glazes and the dust produced by rubbing-back can seriously damage the lungs. If you're sharpening tools on your grindstone, protective goggles are another must.

Certain basic safety measures should be in effect at all times in your workspace.
I have already suggested that the kiln should be installed not too

far from the workbench, so as to avoid having to carry heavy and sometimes fragile pieces over longish distances.
The ideal in fact would be that the kiln be situated outside the work area, especially if it runs on gas. Firing can generate certain highly volatile and/or toxic vapours; explosions and cases of asphyxiation are not unknown in the studios of unwary practitioners.
If your kiln is installed inside your studio, be absolutely sure that the ventilation system meets the guidelines laid down by the manufacturer.

As far as questions of electricity are concerned, the fact that the floor is often wet – and that your hands and tools are constantly in touch with water – means that all wiring, switches and leads should be in perfect condition.
And even so, get into the habit of drying your hands before you turn on a machine, a light, your kiln and so on.
Better safe than sorry – an old and oft-repeated adage, but one that can save lives. And when the life in question is your own…

5. *Working with Moulds*

Now that we're about to go into the business of successfully producing agateware pieces in more detail, we need to take a look at a part of the standard equipment which for us will be as indispensable as the wheel is for the traditional potter: the mould. Press-moulding and hump-moulding, the two main variants of the technique – at least in the present context –

Press-moulds and hump-moulds.

are virtually as old as the art of pottery itself. The Chinese tradition includes the use of moulds since its very beginnings – and this is also the case for the Indian potters of precolumbian America. The embalmers of ancient Egypt took moulds of the faces of the Pharaohs and their families after their death. The death masks that have come down to us from this distant era are without doubt the oldest plaster objects in the world. Plaster: throughout the long history of art we find this material ever-present, in the work not only of ceramicists, but also of our greatest sculptors. Working with plaster demands a skill out of the ordinary – even today, in the building trade the 'humble' plasterer is a highly respected specialist! But the efforts it requires are balanced out by the rewards: notably the capacity to reproduce the most complex shapes and the most delicate textures. Few contemporary ceramicists in fact produce their own moulds, preferring to work up a model of the shape or object they want to reproduce, then handing the model over to a specialist mould-maker.

Plaster is really only gypsum (calcium sulphate) that has been

Below: *Two views of a bowl after demoulding.*

Right: *Preparing an inlay plate on a hump-mould.*

ground up, then heated to 150°. It's hard to imagine a material better suited to the making of moulds. Its preparation and utilisation demand a considerable finesse: it's a delicate substance – and yet we all know how tough and intransigent plaster is once it has set.

In as far as the use of plaster moulds in the field of agateware is concerned, we quite simply need them all the time. This is because, even though the forms and objects that interest us are simple, they don't lend themselves to being turned on a wheel, or to the other standard manual procedures. At the same time, let's not forget that this highly specific way of working gives us the possibility of unique design and colour effects. The most popular pieces are dishes, plates, ashtrays, bowls and vases. All very simple objects, but sometimes they call for moulds comprising several pieces – and obviously the pieces have to fit together with no margin for error. It's not difficult to see why so many potters opt for getting someone else to make their moulds for them! A case where the shoemaker is well-advised to stick to his last.

The pouring of a plaster mould is effected using a model made of clay, of wood or of any other material that is not likely to lose its shape when it comes into contact with the wetness of the plaster. Here too, it can be a good idea to get a specialist in: getting the original model right isn't easy either – and a mould made from a defective or

inaccurate model is no good to anybody. If however, you want to try your hand at making your own moulds, it's not impossible. I would simply advise you to buy a book on the subject first: most specialist shops stock a selection. So – we're going to be working with a press-mould (which is concave) and a hump-mould (which is convex). Each of them can take a slab of clay prepared in advance to the specifications of the project you have in mind.

And now, after several chapters of theory and talking, everything is coming together – the moulds, the coloured slip, the slabs of clay wrapped in a damp cloth, the tools laid out ready for use – and our imagination is fired up. At last we're going to let our creativity loose and start making some agateware pieces. After all, that's what we're here for!

In the author's studio: plenty of storage space for the moulds.

6. *Marbling*

Preparing a marbled motif

I'd like to start with an example of a marbled motif in four colours.
Firstly, as explained earlier (see page 22), you'll need to prepare several 'balls' of different-coloured clay – about the size of a tennis ball will do.

We're going to make our marbled motif in the same way as you roll out the pastry to make a tart – and in a series of simple steps, illustrated on the following pages:

A delightful combination of a flower-motif and various marblings.

– Take the ball of white clay (for example), wedge it, knead it and then roll it out with the rolling pin.
– Repeat the operation for the green ball, then the red one, the navy blue one… Now stack the coloured slabs one on top of the other.
– Using the flat of your hand, firmly strike the layered block you've just created, so as to expel the air bubbles and flatten it out a little.
– With the cutting wire, cut the block of clay in two and put one piece on top of the other.
– Then repeat the operation.

The more often you repeat the cutting, the finer the striping on the cross-section will be. Now, using the cutting wire, cut fine lengthwise layers along the block: these should be 2 or 3 mm thick for inlay work and 7 or 8 mm for a motif of the same thickness as the slab. Take the layers you've just cut, place them flat on your marble work-surface and roll them up so as to make a solid clay cylinder.

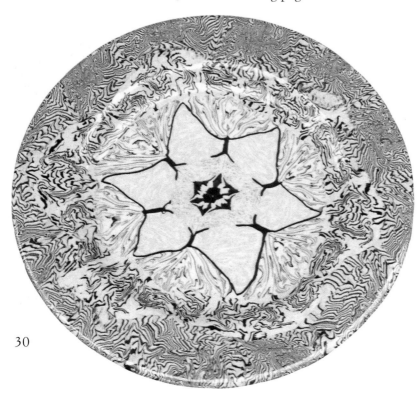

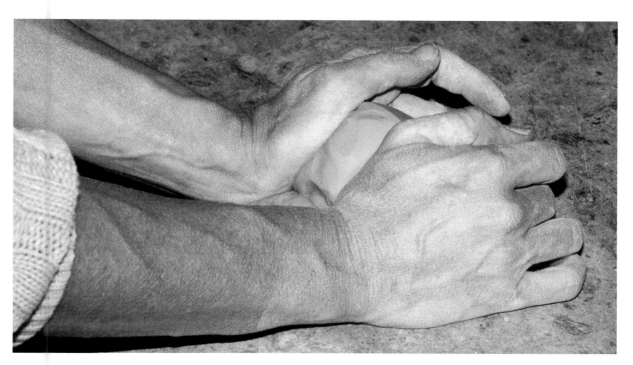

1. Wedging the ball of clay: to expel all the air bubbles you need to strike the ball vigorously on a table several times, turning it a little in your hands after each blow.

2. After the wedging, meticulously kneading the clay will give it greater plasticity.

3. Left: *Repeat the operation for the other balls of coloured clay, then flatten each one with the rolling pin. The number and choice of colours used is up to you.*

5. Below: *Cut the block in two with the cutting wire – then stack the two blocks, strike them and flatten them as before.*

4. Above: *The coloured slabs are stacked one on top of the other. Now you will need to strike the block with the flat of your hand, to expel the air bubbles and to flatten it slightly.*

6. Above: *The new block is also cut in two, and the pieces are stacked, flattened – and once more cut in two. The finer you want the striping to be, the more often you'll have to repeat this operation.*

7. Right: *Take your cutting wire and section the blocks lengthwise into layers. The layers shoud be 2-3 mm thick for surface inlays, and 7-8 mm thick for a motif going right through the slab.*

33

8, 9. Line the layers up widthwise on a smooth, flat surface – a sheet of marble, for example – then roll them up to make a solid cylinder of clay.

11. Below: *The marbled interior of the clay cylinder.*

10. Above: *The clay cylinder will have to be compressed until you get the diameter you want for the piece you have in mind.*

First variation: Tight marbling

Once the cylinder of multicoloured clay has been prepared, the marbling is already there, hidden inside it. All you have to do to make it visible is cut the cylinder in cross-section.

– Stand your clay cylinder on end and working from the top down, cut it into slices. For the project we have in mind here – a bowl – each slice is going to be about 7 mm thick. Bear in mind that the overall diameter of the cylinder should be 12 to 13 cm, corresponding to that of the bowl.

– Enlarge the slice slightly by running the rolling pin over it. Just as when you're working from a sewing pattern, you have to allow about 1 cm extra along the edges. For example, if your bowl is going to be 12 cm wide, the slice should be 13-14 cm wide, to be sure that it will completely cover the inside of the mould. All you have to do now is set your clay into the press-mould.

For your marbled pieces the work must first be allowed to dry (3-5 days), then rubbed back with steel wool so as to bring out the motifs clearly.

1. Firstly, make a cylinder of marbled clay, as described on pages 30-35. The cylinder should be 12 to 13 cm in diameter, so as to match accurately the dimensions of the piece you are going to make. Above, we see a slice taken from the cylinder, with the press-mould to be used for the bowl.

2. Here we see the piece of clay being lifted off, after cutting with the slicer. The slice should be about 7 mm thick.

3. The slice should be made slightly wider than the diameter of the bowl by running the rolling pin over it: for a bowl 12 cm in diameter, you will need a slice of clay of around 13-14 cm in diameter.

4. The slice of clay is placed in the mould. The mould is then centred on the banding wheel and held in place with pieces of clay.

5. Turn the banding wheel, pressing on the clay with a damp sponge so as to force it exactly into the shape of the mould.

6. Once the piece is dry, rubbing back with steel wool brings out the marbled motif in all its clarity.

Facing page: *Detail of the plate shown on page 30.*

Second variation: Loose marbling

N.B. For loose marbling, make sure the striping is not too fine.

First off, you'll need to repeat the operation described on the preceding pages for the first stages of the preparation of a tightly marbled clay (see photos 1-5, pages 31-32). Then the process is as follows:

– Having made up the marbled clay block in the same way as before, cut it into two sections. Lightly work these sections with your hands; this will spread the tight marbling somewhat. Then make up your block again and divide it up into slices 7 mm thick. For this and the subsequent parts of the operation, see photos 1-6.

– Take the press-mould, centre it on the banding wheel and fix it securely in place with pieces of clay. Using both hands, set one of the slices carefully in the mould and press it precisely into place. To make sure the clay meets the inside of the mould all over, press on it with a damp sponge, turning the banding wheel as you go.

For obvious reasons we've chosen to start with a simple piece, but the same basic principle can be applied to

1. Cut a block of striped clay into two pieces.

2. The piece on the left has been slightly flattened out.

much more complex objects. In these latter cases, the way of working remains the same, but the manipulations involved are more complex.

Once you've acquired the basic principles, keep practising; when you feel ready, try yourself out on a range of more demanding pieces: vases, candlesticks, lamp bases and so on.

3. Roll the flattened piece back over on itself, lengthwise. Then do the same for the other half.

4. Place the two pieces one on top of the other and pack them down – but without handling the clay more than is necessary.

5. Cut in two, the resultant block reveals the loose marbling inside.

6. Flatten the slab of clay with the rolling pin until you get the desired diameter.

A superb example of the loose marbling technique.

7. Geometrical Patterns

For our first look at the different styles of decoration used by the creators of agateware, it seemed more than logical to begin with the two main types of marbling.

Not only are marbled patterns the most traditional of all in this field, they also help the beginner to understand the part played by chance; marbling illustrates perfectly the fine balance between inspiration and accident, and the way the two can combine to give truly magnificent results.

Thus the potter also becomes an explorer, setting out in search of new forms – and of a beauty which is to be discovered and laid bare, at least as much as it is to be created.

This exploration is a fascinating, ongoing process, and one whose results become more and more striking as the potter progressively masters his craft. Now we're going to explore the technique of superimposed layers: and here we find, in the realm of geometrical patterns, a range of possibilities of an absolutely stunning richness.

This ashtray by Mireille de Reilhan illustrates one of the many possibilities of geometrical patterns.

First variation: Striping

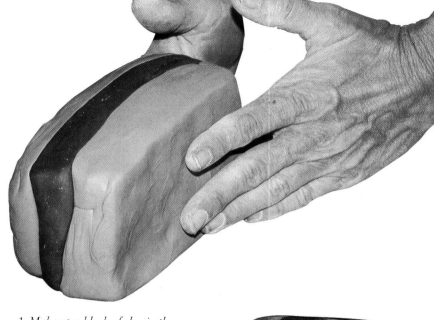

Here we're dealing with the simplest and the most elementary of all the geometrical types of patterning.

– As with marbling, start with a block of colours. Three will do to begin with: dark blue, light blue and white. The procedure is the same for marbling, at least inasfar as the initial operations are concerned.

– When you've finished stacking up the layers you've cut with your wire, turn the block of clay on its side. The stripes are ready.

– Using the cutting wire again, cut off several layers and lay them down flat one beside the other, on a sheet of plastic film. Cover them with a second sheet of plastic, then lightly run the rolling pin over them lengthwise; this will stop the pattern losing its shape as you work. Thus you end up with a striped slab of clay that can be used with a press-mould or a hump-mould, according to the object you have in mind.

1. Make up a block of clay in three colours: light blue, dark blue and white.

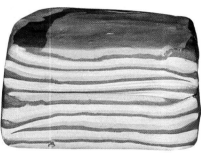

2. Prepare a striped block, following the instructions in the chapter on marbling. Then pack down.

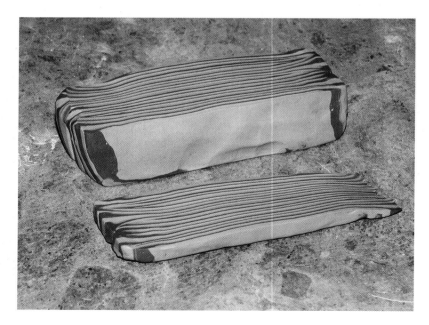

3. Turn the block on its side and using your wire, cut it into slices about 5 mm thick.

44

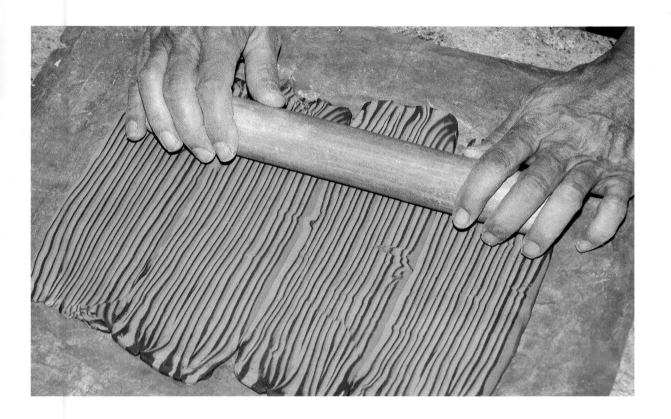

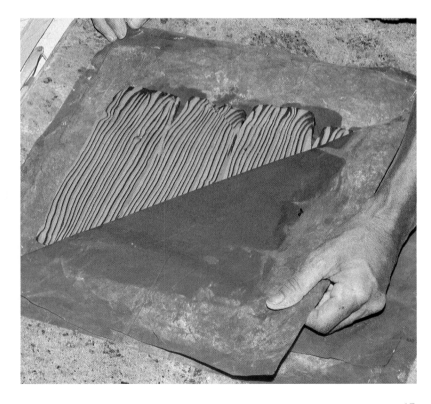

4. Place the slices one beside the other on a sheet of plastic film – this is to stop them sticking to the workbench. Cover them with another sheet of plastic – once again to stop them sticking – then flatten them out a little with the rolling pin.

5. Here we see the slab of clay set in place on a hump-mould, prior to being pressed into the desired shape. For the exact way of working, see Chapter 8 and the photos on pages 66-67.

Second variation: Weaving

To begin, you will need to prepare two striped blocks of clay, as shown in the preceding chapters.

It's important that your weaving motifs should be clear and 'easy to read', so I suggest that for a start you limit yourself to two contrasting colours: blue and white, for example.

– Now place the two blocks one on top of the other, but with the stripes running in different directions (see photo 2, p. 48).

– Now you have a single block of clay. In order to make the two parts adhere firmly, strike the block vigorously down on the table a couple of times – but without flattening it too much.

– Turn the block on its side: don't forget that it's the end of the block that actually shows the motif you've created.

– Use your knife to cut the block into slices, then put the slices side by side to make up a slab. You can use this slab as you see fit.

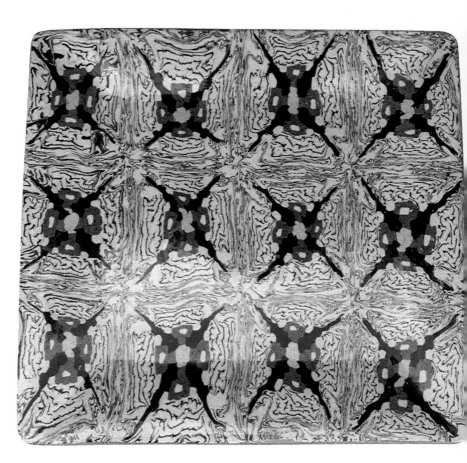

This ashtray by Mireille de Reilhan is based on the repetition of a single geometrical motif.

1. Prepare a striped block of clay (as explained in the preceding chapters), using 2 or 3 contrasting colours. Cut the block lengthwise into two equal parts.

2. Place one half of the block on the workbench with the stripes vertical. Then place the second half on top of the first, with the stripes running horizontally. Pack down lightly, to ensure the adhesion of the two parts.

3. Turn the block on its side and cut it into slices about 4-5 mm thick.

4. Arrange the slices on a piece of plastic, alternating them as shown in the photo. Cover them with another sheet of plastic, then join them together via a light overall pressure with the rolling pin.

5. The end result: a 'woven' motif that
you will be able to use with the mould
of your choice.

50

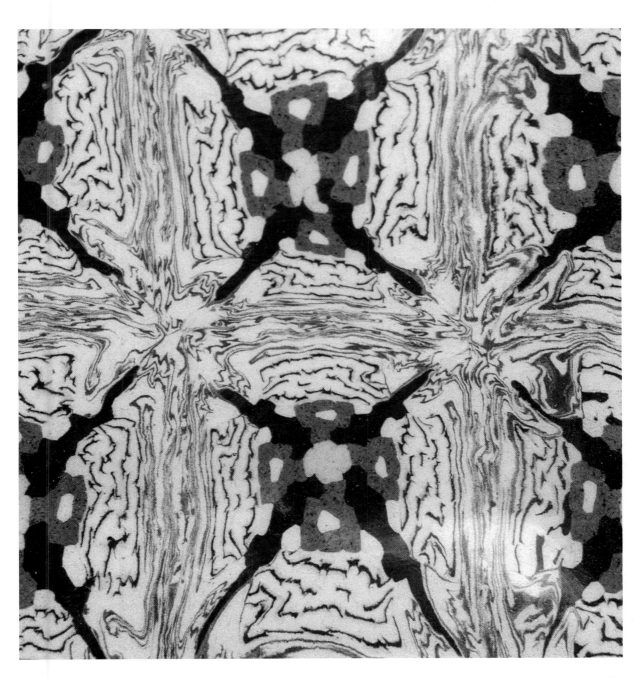

Third variation:
Feathering

We're going to look now at the technique known as 'feathering'. This type of motif is highly prized in Japan, and certain Japanese potters have brought the technique to an extraordinary level of delicacy and refinement.

– Begin with the preparation of a striped block of clay, just as you did for the woven motif. At this stage it's a good idea to use no more than two colours.

– Make yourself a 'slice of stripes', following the procedure described on p. 44.

– At this point you have two possibilities:

a) Either you place this striped layer of clay (2 mm thick) on a slab of white clay (approximately 5 mm thick), thus using the white clay as a base.

b) Or you opt initially for cutting a thicker slice of the striped clay (say 7 mm), with the aim of creating a piece which will show the motif on both sides.

– Start turning the layer of striped clay over and over on itself (see photo 2, opposite page), following the direction of the stripes. You will once more end up with a block of clay that will need to be flattened by being vigorously struck on the workbench.

– Turn the block on edge.

– Using your cutting wire, cut the block once more into slices, then place the slices one beside the other. Thus you will create a slab whose finely varied motif evokes the plumage of a bird.

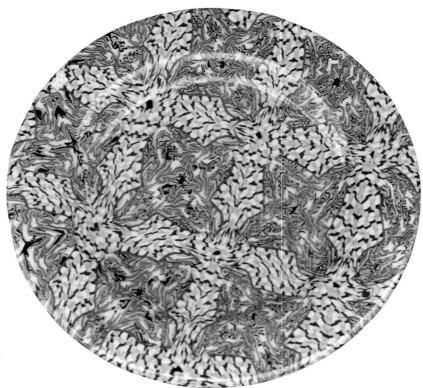

Mireille de Reilhan: This plate illustrates the visual complexity that comes with hard work and experience.

1. Prepare a narrowly-striped slab of clay. In this example three colours have been used.

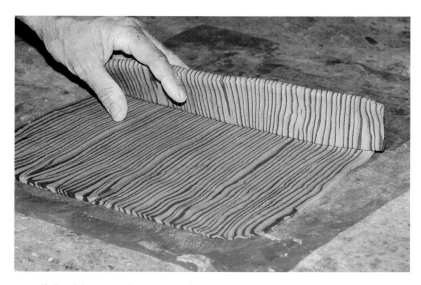

2. Roll the slab over and over on itself, following the direction of the stripes (as shown in this photo).

5. Right: *Place the layers one beside the other on a piece of plastic. Cover them with another piece of plastic, to avoid sticking, then join the sections into a slab by running the rolling pin lightly over the surface.*

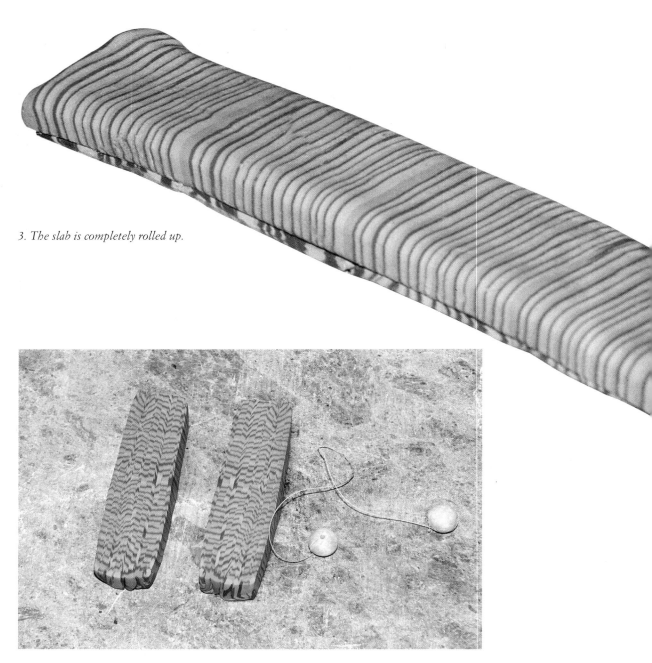

3. The slab is completely rolled up.

4. Working lengthwise, cut the slab into layers 4-5 mm thick.

6. Lay the slab on a hump-mould and press it firmly into place with a damp sponge.

7. Cut off the superfluous clay around the edges and allow to dry. For the finishing-off, see the section on Inlay, in Chapter 8.

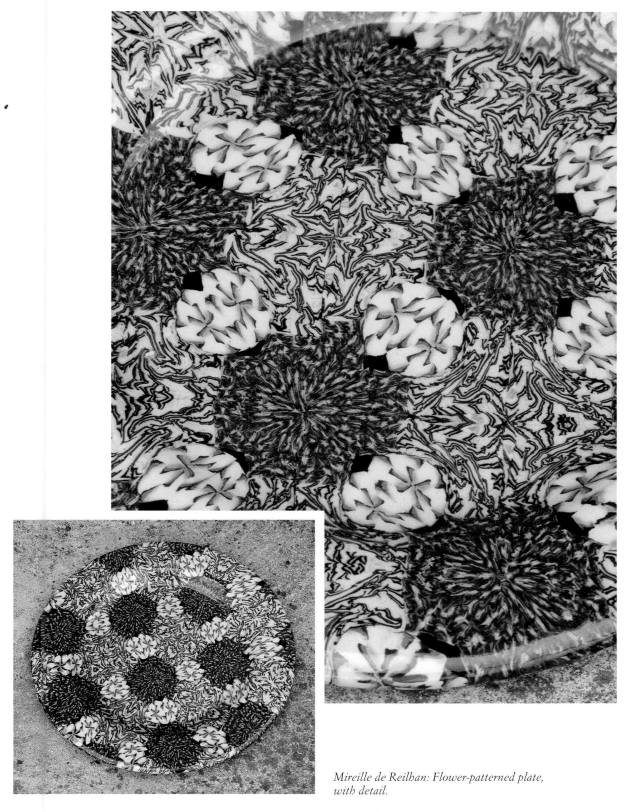

Mireille de Reilhan: Flower-patterned plate,
with detail.

Fourth variation: Checkerboard effects

Here again we are dealing with a geometrical motif much appreciated by connoisseurs and yet surprisingly simple to execute: the checkerboard.

- First off, make a series of clay 'sausages' (as for a coil pot) in blue and white.
- Stack them one on top of the other, alternating the colours as you go.
- Pack them down, turn them on edge, cut them into slices and assemble them into a slab, as you've been doing in the preceding exercises.

And now what?

From here on in, it's up to you. The four geometrical approaches described here are not especially complicated – but the possibilities they offer as to size, use of colour, different arrangements of their elements, and so on, are practically infinite. And there are other motifs and approaches – many, many others. So, as I've just said, it's up to you to imagine them, invent them, discover them, dream them up – and then make them…

A good potter knows that sometimes he needs a daring variation to set off the overall motif of a piece.

1. Using a series of clay 'sausages' (as for a coil pot), prepare a block of stripes in two colours: navy blue and white, for example. Then, as in the preceding exercises, cut the block into striped layers about 4-5 mm thick.

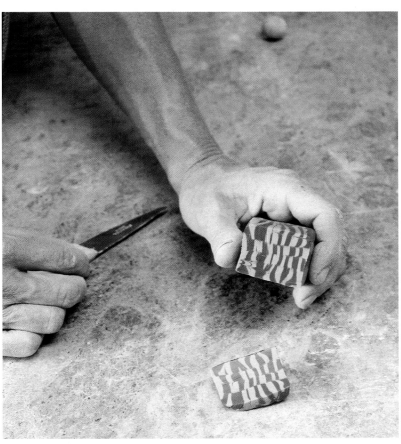

2. Stack the layers one on top of the other, alternating the direction of the stripes, then cut the block thus created into slices.

3. Place the slices side by side on a sheet of plastic, and cover them with a second sheet.

4. Force the slices together with the pressure of the rolling pin. The result will be a slab that you'll be able to adapt to a whole range of projects.

8. Inlay Techniques

This technique is very closely related to agateware. So much so that we could describe inlay as simply a sophisticated variation of the main subject of this book. There are also interesting similarities with the marquetery of skilled cabinet makers.

The word 'inlay' gives in fact a brief but clear description of the technique: what's initially involved is the creation of motifs of all kinds – they can be figurative or abstract – in clays that have been coloured with metallic oxydes; these motifs are then inserted ('inlaid') into a slab of clay of a different colour. Once dry, the surface is carefully scraped back with a rubber kidney, then meticulously 'sanded' with steel wool or a jex pad – processes which bring out the shapes and colour contrasts in all their splendour. The ceramicist using inlay techniques has at his disposal an almost infinite choice of possibilities. All the classic (and less classic) subjects – birds, flowers, fish, landscapes, etc. – await his attention; and when he has prepared his coloured clays, designed and cut out his motifs, decided on the arrangement that best expresses his artistic intentions – then he can create on the surface of his clay slab a work of art as exact as anything painted with a brush.

By adding a simple transparent glaze he can then maximize its sheen and the play of light on its surface.

The only real problem likely to crop up is the appearance of cracks in the finished work. This is usually due to the inlaid motifs, which shrink more than the clay in which they have been set. You can eliminate this risk almost entirely by adding whiting or a fine grog (clay which has been biscuit-fired then ground up) to the clay used for the decorative elements. The addition of a grog reduces the shrinkage that takes place during firing.

The ephemeral beauty of butterflies, captured forever in this plate created by Mireille de Reilhan.

Their beauty of form and their lively colours have made butterflies one of Mireille de Reilhan's favourite subjects.

A simple inlay motif: The 'deck of cards' plate

In this section we're going to take an example of inlay which will be easy for the beginner to execute – and which presents the added advantage of letting him also put into practice the geometric and marbling techniques already worked on in the preceding chapters.

– Begin by preparing a slab of marbled clay 5 mm thick, and store it for the time being under plastic – in a rubbish bag, for example!
– Now prepare a block of 'little squares' (see the preceding chapter on the Checkerboard motif), and cut it into slices about 5 mm thick.
– Take each slice and transform it into a specific shape of your own choosing – a heart, for example – using either a sharp cutting instrument or, for maximum precision, a pastry-cutter.
– Then, back to the slab of marbled clay. Enlarge it slightly by running the rolling pin over it, then cut shapes into here and there, preferably using the same pastry-cutter as for the previous step. Now you can fill the 'holes' in the slab with the individual shapes and thus create your pattern.
– Taking your rolling pin again, lightly run it over the slab so as to make the shapes an integral part of the whole. With a little patience and imagination, in this way you can achieve astonishingly beautiful results.
– Lay the slab carefully on a hump-mould, making sure that the side into which you inserted the individual shapes is face-down on the mould.
– Centre the mould accurately on the banding-wheel, fix it into place, then turn the wheel, smoothing the slab down into shape with a damp sponge.

As you work on the banding wheel, you'll see your motif (which is visible on both sides of the slab) gradually disappear under a film of moist clay. Don't panic! Once the piece has dried thoroughly, a rub-down with steel wool will bring the motif back to the surface, just as it was before.

> **For all inlay work, just as for the other techniques described in this book, you'll have to allow 3 to 5 days for drying-out, before you can really 'polish up' your motifs with steel wool. For details, see the section on Drying, in Chapter 9.**

1. Prepare a solid cylinder of loose-marbled red and white clay (see Chapter 6), about 5 mm thick.

2. *Make up a round slab of the desired diameter, without forgetting that it should be slightly wider than the mould you're going to use.*

4. Right: *Cut out a selection of shapes in the marbled slab, using your range of pastry-cutters. Then fill the holes with the same shapes, cut out of the checkerboard slab with the same pastry-cutters.*

3. *Prepare a slab along the lines of the checkerboard motif (see Chapter 7), about 5 mm thick. Make sure you've got the pastry-cutters for the shapes you want to inlay.*

5. Using your rolling pin, compress the slab very slightly – just enough to set the motifs firmly in place without deforming them.

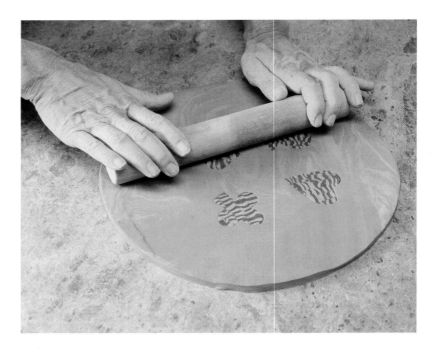

6. Set up the hump-mould on the banding-wheel, fix it securely in place, then carefully lay the completed slab over it. Press into place with a damp sponge.

7. Prepare a little clay 'sausage' to use for the base of the plate. Set the banding-wheel in motion and put the base in place.

8. The plate is almost finished. Keep the banding-wheel turning, and smooth the surface down with a rubber kidney.

9. The 'deck of cards' plate in its finished state.

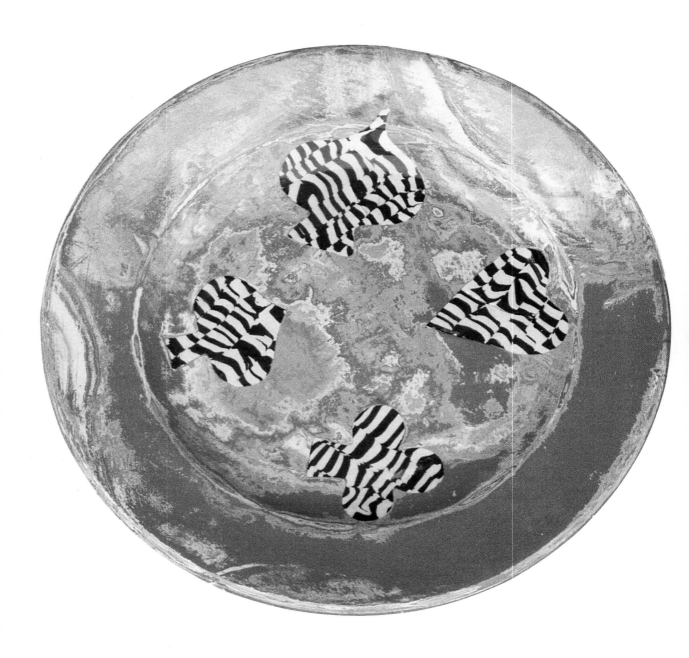

Right: *There are more things in this world than butterflies and decks of cards. Fish are another excellent subject for inlay work.*

Below: *The same plate seen in close-up.*

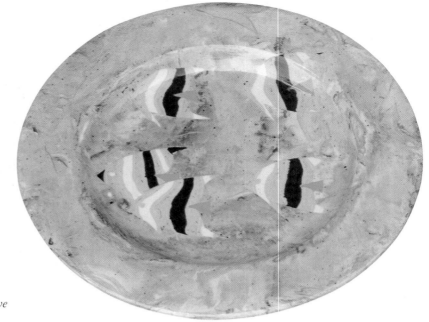

Right: *Here we note the use of relatively widely-spaced bands of coloured clay. Don't be afraid to introduce this kind of variety into your own work.*

Below: *This detail from the plate above shows the precision that characterizes the work of Mireille de Reilhan.*

In every art-form, variety is the spice of life. Don't let yourself get into a rut where your subjects and techniques are concerned. Take a lesson from the author of this book, whose work involves a constant search for innovation, in terms both of her subjects and her ways of approaching them.

9. Drying, Glazing, Firing

Drying

Some things in this world are a lot trickier than they look; drying out your pots once you've made them falls right into this category.

In the course of describing the creation of the various pieces appearing in these pages, we've tried to emphasize the meticulousness needed to successfully bring an agateware piece to the drying stage. Here we are with a delicate layer of clay neatly fitted against the inside (or the outside) of its mould: after drying and firing, this shape is going to become a delicately marbled bowl, a plate or an ashtray – if all goes well. Ceramicists are haunted by a terrible fear when they come to the drying and firing stages – the fear of seeing a piece ruined by cracks, fissures, breakages, swellings, bucklings and all the other deformations that can lead to only one place: the junkheap. We're going to look at the question of firing further on. Before we do, let's worry about the business of getting your pieces dry.

To be able to work clay in the way demanded by the techniques outlined in this book, we have to give it the right degree of plasticity. Doing this means that the clay has to contain a considerable quantity of water – up to 30% or 40% of its own weight!– In fact there is always water naturally present in clay – in the form of molecules which are part of its structure, in association with the actual molecules of the clay itself.

This water is removed by firing. There is also the water that gets added to clay in the course of preparation and working. Clay is a naturally absorbent material – much more so than most, in fact – and this absorbency has certain very definite consequences for the potter.

The most notable of these consequences is that during drying, this additional water evaporates, causing the clay to shrink. In order to avoid the cracking, buckling and other undesirable results mentioned above, the drying has to take place slowly and at a constant rate: only thus can we control the progressive coming-together of the individual clay particles during the gradual evaporation of the water separating them. If the evaporation is too rapid, the result inside the clay body is chaos. In a highly humid environment, evaporation will be very slow or non-existent.

Facing page: *After demoulding, the author has set a variety of pieces on her garden wall, to aid the drying process.*

On the other hand, an environment that is too hot or too dry – out in the wind, or in direct sunlight, for example – the evaporation will go ahead much too quickly.

For these very good reasons, during drying we have to keep each of our creations in a dry, sheltered environment – then take it out of its mould at the right moment.

A piece is sufficiently dry to be demoulded when it can be loosened by a series of light, rapid taps on the outside of the mould with the heel of the hand.

Once it has been demoulded, it should immediately be wrapped in a sheet of plastic and set on a piece of wood to dry further; this second part of the process will take another 2 or 3 days. Once the drying has been brought to completion in this way, it only remains to rub the piece back, in order to bring out the motif and get rid of the surface imperfections.

Glazing

When a potter successfully gets a piece to the firing stage, he's reached that magic moment when his capacities are finally going to be shown up for what they are. But once he has dried the piece in question, there remains a further intermediate stage: glazing. In the agateware context, glazing presents no great problems, but it deserves your close attention all the same.

– The basic approach consists in using a transparent glaze which will accentuate the various colours used and the outlines of the motifs. At the same time it renders the piece

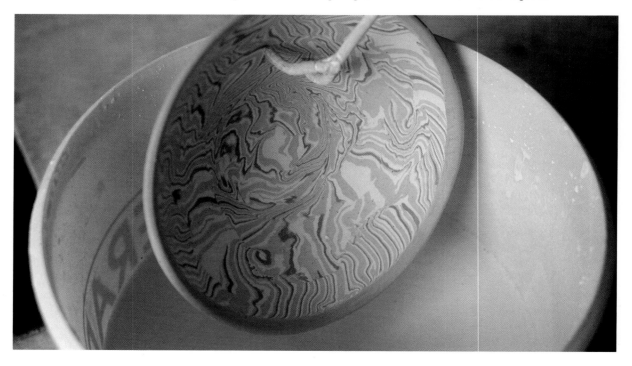

White at the outset, the glaze will be transparent after firing.

impermeable – no mean consideration in the case of vases, plates, bowls and so on.

– All we do, really, is cover the entire surface of the piece with liquid glaze – most often by holding the piece with a special pair of tongs and simply dipping it. But first the piece has to be biscuited (given an initial firing) – and after glazing it will be fired again.

– The glaze is a silicon compound chemically related to glass. During the second firing the glaze vitrifies and renders the piece impermeable.

– Obviously, glazing by dipping is only practicable for relatively small pieces. If you work on a larger scale, you'll need to brush or spray your glaze. There are different methods of spraying, so you'll need to check with your pottery shop to find out which one best suits your needs. All spraying processes necessitate the wearing of a mask.

– If, as is sometimes the case, a biscuit-fired piece turns out to be extremely porous, you can cut down its absorption of liquid glaze by first soaking it with water. This applies whether you're going to dip-glaze or spray.

Firing

The great English potter Bernard Leach once remarked that 'the potter's life is indelibly marked by the anxiety that goes with firing, for he knows that in those few hours all the work that has gone before is going to be put to the test'. In other words, this highly delicate operation requires a prior level of know-how and technical competence for which 'near enough is *never* good enough'. Firing takes place in two stages:

The first (or biscuit) firing
The ideal temperatures for the first firing are as follows:

For red terra cotta:
1000 – 1180 °C
For white terra cotta:
1060 – 1140 °C
For stoneware: 1200 – 1300 °C
For porcelain: 1280 – 1350 °C

When a pot emerges from the first firing, it is still porous. The distinctive texture it has at this stage is the origin of the term 'biscuit' firing.

Second Firing
Between the two firings the glazing of the piece takes place. In the course of the second firing, the glaze covering the piece is subjected to intense heat: if the temperature is sufficiently high – between 1250 and 1400 °C – the glaze takes on the consistency of glass. At this temperature it's no longer question of a simple coating of the kind we find on stoneware or terra cotta: the glaze actually combines chemically with the clay. Having said all this, we need to be clear as to the situation in respect of the low-firing clays used for agateware. As a general rule the second firing is used simply to harden the glaze; in

other words the role of the glaze here is basically a decorative and æsthetic one. This means that a low-temperature firing – at around 980 °C – will do the necessary, but without providing any guarantee as to the impermeability of the glazed surface. Whatever the case, when you buy ready-to-use clays and glazes – which is the case for most potters, whether they're beginners or not – the firing temperature is always indicated on the label.

Single firing

In addition to the fairly standard two-firing approach, there's always the possibility of glazing a piece in its raw state (without a prior biscuiting), and then giving it a single, definitive firing. The difficulty is that handling a raw piece during glazing, and then getting it into the kiln without damaging it poses all sorts of practical problems; all things considered, this is not a very economical way of doing things.

There's another major drawback here, in that the firing of glazed, non-biscuited pieces often generates breakages and irreparable blistering of the clay or the glaze.

In addition, since our aim in creating agateware pieces is to produce something lasting, the fragility of single-fired pieces is another argument in favour of the two-firing process.

Kilns

The electric kiln

The heating system in an electric kiln is based on a network of elements arranged in a special way inside the firing chamber. The firebricks that line the inside of the kiln are there to stop the heat from escaping and to ensure a gradual accumulation of heat that will allow the potter to fire his pieces at the correct temperature.

Gas-fired kilns

Gas-fired kilns use a system of gas burners inside the firing chamber to bring the temperature up to the different levels needed by the various clays and techniques.

The wood-fired kiln

Here we're talking about what is by far the oldest and most traditional method of firing pots. The heat source is wood or some other natural combustible material. The wood-fired kiln is not all that convenient – it requires constant surveillance

in respect of the fuel and the temperature level – but it is still used by some potters. This is largely because the results it gives fit in with the investigation of new and traditional textures and decors that loom large in the work of a growing number of ceramicists.

A word in closing…

The kiln, for the dedicated potter, is the tool par excellence: after all, ceramics is the art of clay that has been heated intensely – fired, as we so accurately say.

Thus each encounter with the kiln is the moment of truth.

The kiln, so to speak, is the cocoon within which the chrysalis undergoes its strange metamorphosis; and all the while the craftsman is there, fingers crossed, waiting for the new creature to take flight when the door of the kiln is opened. And this new creature is the work of art, however modest it might be.

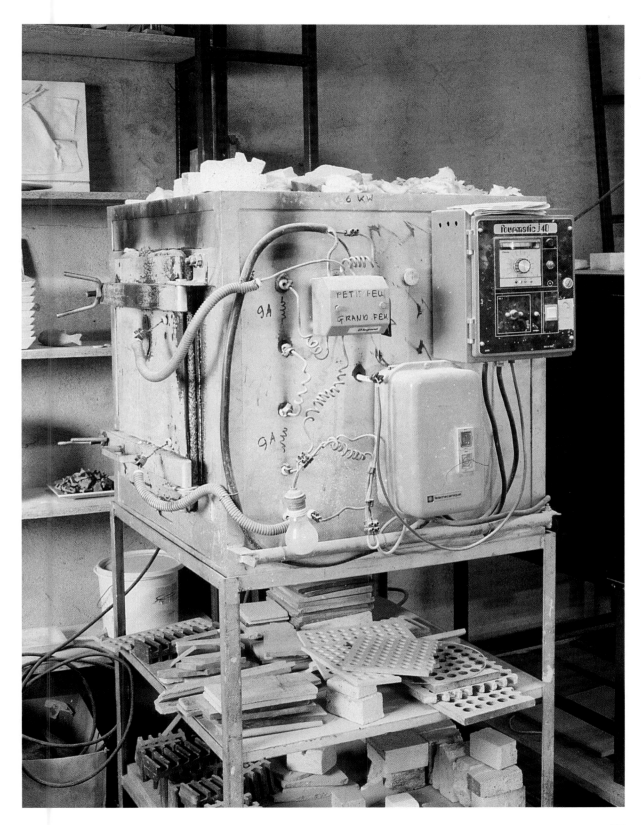

Postface

'There's something magical about all this', Mireille de Reilhan says of her work. And she invites us to let ourselves 'be seduced by the unexpected' and to 'make our dreams out of what chance throws up to us'.

Then there's the kiln, which for her calls up the image of the chrysalis – the chrysalis from which the brilliantly coloured butterfly will burst forth.

Just a butterfly? Nothing more? Just a modest work of art? And the potter, this poet-technician, this patient explorer who sets off in search of new forms: what is he really looking for – or to put it more simply, what is he also looking for? Have you ever watched a potter – a ceramic artist – at work?

There's nothing grandiloquent about his gestures, there are no high-flown words. Just a sort of inner quietude, a serenity, a tranquil determination.

There's something in this that makes you think of a peasant at work, or of someone making a long journey on foot – a man who knows that whatever you do you need to take good care of your means of doing it. His moments of delighted amazement, like his moments of anxiety, are guarded – not because he's half-hearted, but out of necessity.

He knows that the excitement, the sound and the fury a painter or a musician can permit himself are not for him. And in any case, they suit neither him nor his art. He knows too that this art leaves no room for approximation, nor for showing-off.

The technical demands to which he so willingly submits are an integral part of what he has set out to do. I'm not referring simply to the practical side of his work, but also to what, without pretentiousness, we could call his inner quest.

It happens sometimes that he makes room in his work for chance and for the accidental –